AMAZING BASKETBALL RECORDS

BY PAUL HOBLIN

Published by The Child's World®
1980 Lookout Drive • Mankato, MN 56003-1705
800-599-READ • www.childsworld.com

Acknowledgments
The Child's World®: Mary Berendes, Publishing Director
The Design Lab: Design
Amnet: Production
Red Line Editorial: Editorial direction

Design Element: Mark Cinotti/Shutterstock Images

Photographs ©: Paul Vathis/AP Images, Cover, 11;
AP Images, 5, 13, 15, 23; Matt A. Brown/AP Images, 7;
Bettmann/Corbis/AP Images, 9; Fred Jewell/AP Images, 17;
Michael Conro/AP Images, 19; Michael Caulfield/AP
Images, 21; Sue Ogrocki/AP Images, 25; Kathy Willens/AP
Images, 27; Doug Pizac/AP Images, 29.

ISBN 9781614734024
LCCN 2012946497

Printed in the United States of America
Mankato, MN
November, 2012
PA02146

Disclaimer: The information in this book is current
through the 2011-12 NBA season.

ABOUT THE AUTHOR
Paul Hoblin has written several sports books. He has an MFA from the University of Minnesota. He plays many different sports.

TABLE OF
CONTENTS

ONE

FROM THE YMCA TO THE NBA

More than 100 years ago, Dr. James Naismith invented the game of basketball. Naismith worked at a YMCA camp. He wanted to give his campers something to do during the winter when it was too cold to play outside. On January 20, 1892, he nailed two peach baskets onto the wall and handed the campers a soccer ball. This was the first ever basketball game.

The game has changed over the years, though. Back then players were not allowed to bounce the ball. Today, dribbling is one of the most important parts of the game. The basket has changed a lot, too. The first baskets did not have **backboards**, something that all hoops have today. In fact, the baskets did not even have holes at the bottom. Whenever a shot was made, someone had to climb a ladder and take out the ball!

Luckily, there was not a lot of scoring back then. The first game ended with a score of 1–0. Today, National Basketball Association (NBA) teams score around 100 points a game.

SHOT CLOCK
One of the reasons NBA teams score so much is because of the shot clock. Teams are given only 24 seconds to shoot. If they don't shoot by then, the ball goes to the other team. The shot clock was first put in use in the 1954–55 season.

The inventor of basketball, Dr. James Naismith, stands in a field with a ball and a basket, the first equipment used in the game.

SCORING TODAY

NBA players score a lot these days. But almost no one has scored as much as Kobe Bryant did on January 22, 2006. His team, the Los Angeles Lakers, was losing to the Toronto Raptors by 18 points in the third quarter. Bryant was so angry about losing that he would not speak to his teammates.

Instead of talking, he took more shots. He shot three-pointers, jump shots, and layups. By the end of the night, he had taken 46 shots—and most of them went in! Bryant scored 81 points in that game. That is the most points scored by a guard in the history of NBA basketball.

More importantly, his team came back to win the game 122–104. "I've seen some remarkable games," his coach said, "but I've never seen one like that before."

GREAT SCORER
Kobe Bryant led the NBA in scoring in the 2005–06 and 2006–07 seasons.

UNSTOPPABLE
Kevin Durant led the league in scoring for three straight seasons from 2009–10 through 2011–12.

Kobe Bryant (8) of the Los Angeles Lakers drives to the basket for two of his 81 points on January 22, 2006.

TWO

AMAZING BASKETBALL PLAYERS

As incredible as Kobe Bryant's 81 points were, there was another player who scored even more points in a single game: center Wilt Chamberlain. At 7 feet 1 inch tall (2.2 m) and 270 pounds (122.5 kg), Chamberlain was bigger than almost everybody else in the league. He also was more athletic. In high school, he was a great hurdler. In college, he was one of the best high jumpers in the country.

Chamberlain's size, speed, and jumping ability made him almost impossible to guard on the basketball court. On March 2, 1962, Chamberlain was unstoppable. He took 63 shots and made 36 of them. By the end of the third quarter, fans began shouting, "Give it to Wilt! Give it to Wilt!"

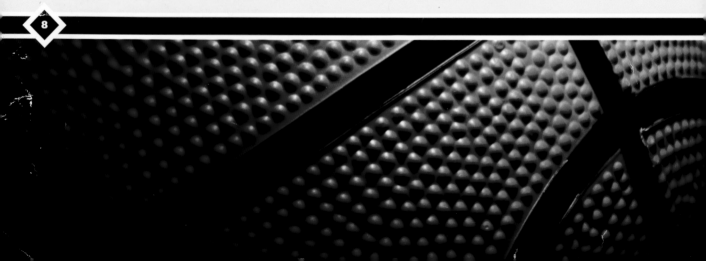

CAREER SCORING CHAMP
Wilt Chamberlain may have had the most points in a single game, but he didn't have the most points all-time. During his 19-year career, Kareem Abdul-Jabbar scored 38,387 points.

At just 17, Wilt Chamberlain was already a track-and-field star at Overbrook High School in Philadelphia.

That is exactly what his teammates did. They kept passing Chamberlain the ball. And he kept scoring. By the end of the game, Chamberlain had scored 100 points. That is the most points ever scored by one player in a single game.

MOST POINTS IN A SINGLE NBA GAME

PLAYER	POINTS	DATE
Wilt Chamberlain	100	March 2, 1962
Kobe Bryant	81	January 22, 2006
Wilt Chamberlain	78	December 8, 1961
David Thompson	73	April 9, 1978
Wilt Chamberlain	73	January 13, 1962
Wilt Chamberlain	73	November 16, 1962

ALL-TIME NBA LEADING SCORERS
1. Kareem Abdul-Jabbar: 38,387
2. Karl Malone: 36,928
3. Michael Jordan: 32,292
4. Wilt Chamberlain: 31,419
5. Kobe Bryant*: 29,484

*Active player as of 2012

Wilt Chamberlain of the Philadelphia Warriors rests in the locker room after he scored 100 points against the New York Knickerbockers on March 2, 1962.

FANTASTIC FREE THROW SHOOTERS

In Wilt Chamberlain's 100-point game, he made 28 of 32 free throws. Usually, Chamberlain was not a very good free throw shooter. But he made most of the shots that day.

The best free throw shooters rarely miss. For a long time, the player with the best free throw **percentage** was Rick Barry. Incredibly, he shot his free throws underhanded. Barry would hold the ball in both hands below his waist, then flip the ball toward the basket.

There are now a couple of players with better free throw percentages than Barry. But no other player shoots his free throws underhanded.

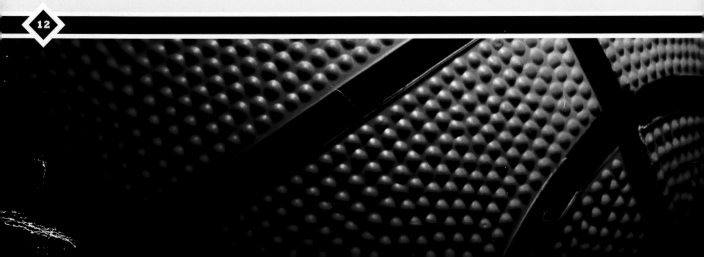

BEST FREE THROW PERCENTAGE
(NBA CAREER)

1. **Mark Price:** 90.39
2. **Steve Nash*:** 90.35
3. **Rick Barry:** 89.98
4. **Peja Stojakovic:** 89.48
5. **Ray Allen*:** 89.39

*Active players as of 2012

Rick Barry, of the
San Francisco Warriors,
grabs a rebound
ball in a game on
December 9, 1966.

NOT JUST A TALL PERSON'S GAME

NBA players are usually really tall. Most are well above 6 feet (1.8 m), and many are more than 7 feet (2.1 m) tall. But short people can play, too. At 5 feet 6 inches (1.7 m), Spud Webb was one of the all-time shortest NBA players.

Webb could jump really high. He was even able to **dunk** a basketball. In 1986, he won the NBA's slam dunk competition. He threw down 360-degree jams. He bounced the ball off the backboard and caught it at the top of his jump. Before his last dunk, the crowd chanted, "Spud, Spud, Spud." He tossed the ball in the air, let it bounce, then grabbed the ball, twisted his body, and slammed the ball through the rim. When he won, he became the shortest player to ever win an NBA slam dunk contest.

MOST ASSISTS (CAREER)

It can be hard for shorter players to score over taller players, but there's more to basketball than scoring. One important skill is an assist. An assist is the pass that leads to a basket. The players with the most career assists are:

14

PLAYER	ASSISTS
John Stockton	15,806
Jason Kidd*	11,842
Mark Jackson	10,334
Earvin "Magic" Johnson	10,141
Steve Nash*	9,916

REBOUNDING
Another important basketball skill is a rebound. That's where a player grabs a missed shot out of the air. The all-time leading rebounder is Wilt Chamberlain. His career rebound record is 23,924.

DOUBLE THREAT
Not only is John Stockton the all-time NBA leader in assists, he's also the all-time leader in steals (3,265)!

Spud Webb jumps high to make a shot over Larry Bird in a 1988 game.

THREE

AMAZING BASKETBALL TEAMS

Before the season, the 1995–96 Chicago Bulls knew they were a good basketball team. They had a new teammate named Dennis Rodman. He was a player who was famous for rebounding and his colorful hair. More importantly, the Bulls had Michael Jordan.

After winning three straight NBA championships, Jordan had retired from basketball in 1993 to play baseball. After a few years, he decided to come back to basketball. Yes, the Bulls knew they would be good in 1995–96. Not only did they win the NBA championship, but their regular-season record (72–10) was also the best in the history of the NBA. And to top it off, Michael Jordan won the Most Valuable Player trophy.

BEST REGULAR-SEASON RECORDS IN THE NBA

SEASON	TEAM	RECORD
1995–96	Chicago Bulls	72–10
1971–72	Los Angeles Lakers	69–13
1996–97	Chicago Bulls	69–13
1966–67	Philadelphia 76ers	68–14
1972–73	Boston Celtics	68–14

SCORING MACHINE

As of 2012, the 1981–82 Denver Nuggets held the highest scoring average of any team in the history of the NBA. The Nuggets scored 126.5 points per game!

17

Chicago Bulls guard Michael Jordan shoots over the Charlotte Hornets during the first quarter of a 1995 game in Chicago.

MOST NBA CHAMPIONSHIPS*

1. Boston Celtics: 17
2. Los Angeles Lakers: 16
3. Chicago Bulls: 6
4. San Antonio Spurs: 4
5. Detroit Pistons: 3
   Golden State Warriors: 3
   Philadelphia 76ers: 3

*Current through 2011–12

WORST TEAM EVER?

After winning his fourth, fifth, and sixth NBA championships, Michael Jordan retired again after the 1997–98 season. Two other stars, Scottie Pippen and Dennis Rodman, also left the Chicago Bulls. That meant that the team went from being one of the best ever to one of the worst—in just one year. They were really bad on April 10, 1999. That day they only scored 49 points against the Miami Heat.

WORST OVERALL RECORDS

As bad as the Bulls were in 1998–99, they do not hold the worst overall record in NBA history. Here are the teams with the most losses in an 82-game schedule.

SEASON	TEAM	LOSSES
1972–73	Philadelphia 76ers	9–73
1992–93	Dallas Mavericks	11–71
1997–98	Denver Nuggets	11–71
1986–87	Los Angeles Clippers	12–70
2009–10	New Jersey Nets	12–70

Indiana Pacers guard Jalen Rose (5) looks to pass in a 1999 game against the Bulls.

IS THERE A LID ON THIS RIM?

The 1998–99 Bulls had serious problems putting the ball in the basket. They had the lowest points-per-game average in NBA history since the league started using the shot clock in 1954: 81.9 points.

BIGGEST HEIGHT DIFFERENCE

At 7 feet 7 inches (2.3 m), Manute Bol was one of the tallest players in NBA history. He was so tall that he could dunk without jumping. In fact, the first time he tried to dunk, he chipped his teeth on the rim.

At 5 feet 3 inches (1.6 m), Muggsy Bogues was the shortest player in NBA history. He was so short that kids sometimes did not realize he was an adult like the rest of the players. "They think *I'm* a little kid out there," Bogues said.

Both men were amazing to watch on the basketball court. But here is something even more amazing: they were teammates. They both played for the Washington Bullets during the 1987–88 season.

TALLEST PLAYERS
- **Manute Bol:** 7 feet 7 inches (2.31 m)
- **Gheorghe Muresan:** 7 feet 7 inches (2.31 m)
- **Yao Ming:** 7 feet 6 inches (2.28 m)
- **Shawn Bradley:** 7 feet 6 inches (2.28 m)

TALL ENOUGH FOR THE MOVIES
Gheorghe Muresan was one of the tallest players in NBA history. He also was one of the tallest actors in movie history. In 1998 he starred in the movie *My Giant.*

Muggsy Bogues drives around Corie Blount of the Los Angeles Lakers during a 1997 game.

SHORTEST PLAYERS

- Muggsy Bogues: 5 feet 3 inches (1.60 m)
- Earl Boykins: 5 feet 5 inches (1.65 m)
- Spud Webb: 5 feet 6 inches (1.68 m)
- Mel Hirsch: 5 feet 6 inches (1.68 m)

FOUR

OTHER AMAZING BASKETBALL RECORDS

Every once in a while, an NBA player breaks a backboard during a game. Usually this happens when a big, strong player dunks really hard. Darryl Dawkins shook and shattered so many backboards that he was known as "Chocolate Thunder." In 1946, Chuck Connors was the first player to break a backboard, but it was not with a slam dunk. He was taking a regular shot. Then, for some reason, the board came crashing down.

23

Darryl Dawkins shatters the backboard during a 1979 game.

PLAYER WHO FOULED OUT THE QUICKEST

NBA players are allowed to commit six **fouls**. After that, the player has to leave the game. Usually players play the whole game without fouling out. But on December 29, 1997, Bubba Wells fouled out of a game in a record three minutes!

FIRST GAME STOPPED BY A BAT

In 2002, Moochie Norris was playing for the Houston Rockets when a bat swooped down and buzzed right by him. Referees stopped the game while the bat soared around the court. Play continued once the bat flew up to the rafters. Later, it swooped down to the court again, and a ball boy caught it with a net.

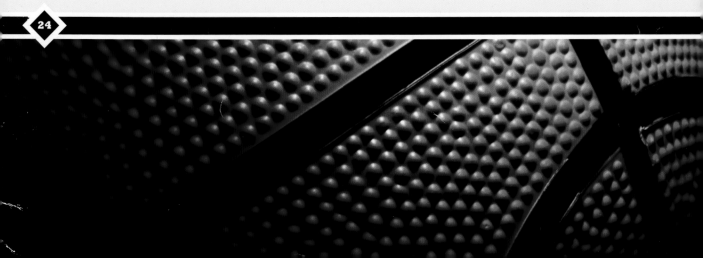

YOUR LAST NAME IS WHAT?

NBA players have their last names written on the backs of their jerseys. In 2011, Ron Artest changed his name to Metta World Peace. Ever since, the back of his jersey has had the unusual last name of *World Peace*.

Los Angeles Lakers forward Metta World Peace huddles with his teammates during a game.

FIRST PLAYER TO BE INJURED
PLAYING A VIDEO GAME

Players are injured on the court all the time. Sometimes these injuries cause players to miss a game (or several games). But during the 1990–91 season, Lionel Simmons was the first to be injured while playing video games. He played so many video games that he hurt both wrists. The injury caused him to miss two NBA games.

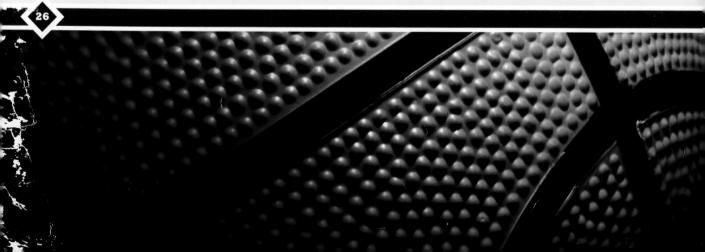

TOO MANY FOULS

In the NBA a player can commit six fouls before he has to leave the game. In college, players only get five fouls before they have to sit on the bench.

Miami Heat forward Glen Rice (41) drives by Sacramento Kings forward Lionel Simmons (22) during a 1991 game.

FIRST PLAYER TO BUY AND EAT FOOD DURING A GAME

At NBA basketball games, fans are encouraged to buy as much food as they want. Players are not. In a 1985 game, Quintin Dailey of the Chicago Bulls got hungry. He had a ball boy bring him a slice of pizza. Then he ate the pizza while he was watching the game from the bench!

STAT STUFFING
A basketball player who gets at least ten of two statistical categories has a "double double." In 2010, Kevin Love had a double double in an amazing 53 straight games. Love scored at least ten points and grabbed at least ten rebounds in each game for almost four months in a row!

Chicago Bulls guard Quintin Dailey shoots a jump shot in the first period of a 1983 game against the Los Angeles Lakers.

GLOSSARY

assist (uh-SISST): An assist is a pass that sets up a basket. John Stockton set an NBA assist record.

backboards (BAK-bordz): Backboards are the hard, flat surfaces behind the basketball hoops. Darryl Dawkins shattered many backboards during games.

dunk (DUNK): A dunk is when a player jumps up and slams the ball down through the basket. Spud Webb was short, but he won the NBA slam dunk contest.

fouls (FOULZ): Fouls are actions that are against the rules of a sport. In the NBA, players who have committed six fouls in a game must sit out.

percentage (pur-SEN-tij): A percentage is a number out of a hundred. Rick Barry once had the best free throw percentage in the NBA.

rebound (RE-bownd): A rebound is when a player gets the ball after a missed shot. Wilt Chamberlain holds the NBA record for career rebounds.

record (REK-urd): To set a record is to do something in a sport that is better than anyone has ever done it before. Kobe Bryant set a scoring record.

steals (STEELZ): Basketball steals happen when the ball is taken away from a player on the other team. John Stockton is the all-time leader in steals.

LEARN MORE

Books

Hareas, John. *Championship Teams.*
New York: Scholastic, 2010.

Ladewski, Paul. *Stars on the Court.* New York: Scholastic, 2009.

Wiseman, Blaine. *Basketball (The Greatest Players).*
New York: Weigl, 2011.

Web Sites

Visit our Web site for links about basketball records:
childsworld.com/links

Note to Parents, Teachers, and Librarians:
We routinely verify our Web links to make sure they are safe and
active sites. So encourage your readers to check them out!

INDEX